THOUGHTS BOOK 1

For Rhyme and Reason

Sandra Trammell Martin

Copyright © 2021 Sandra J. Martin

All rights reserved

The characters and events portrayed in this book are fictitious. Any similarity to real persons, living or dead, is coincidental and not intended by the author.

No part of this book may be reproduced, or stored in a retrieval system, or transmitted in any form or by any means, electronic, mechanical, photocopying, recording, or otherwise, without express written permission of the publisher.

ISBN-13: 9798595164283

Cover design by: Art Painter
Library of Congress Control Number: 2018675309
Printed in the United States of America

CONTENTS

DEDICATION

This book is dedicated to my Mother, Pearl Kiker Trammell, my first encourager and greatest inspiration of a life lived seeking God's Will and exuding His Grace.

I LOVE AND MISS
YOU MOM

MOM

I can picture her childhood sometimes so
clearly as if I had watched her then
I see a child of strength and courage that wanted for some
things but always held dignity her learned friend
She was close to her sisters and so like her Mother, she rivaled her
brothers and obeyed her Father and always knew God was above
Though hard times had fed her in a youth unpolished
she was rich in life with the pride of her family
and the nourishment of their Love
I look at her in sweet admiration for I am a reflection of what I see
I took from her the fire of her youth, the wit of her
tongue, and the need to simply be free
My praise is in that all she has given and
in all that she may have lost
She has never shown the eyes that watch
her the price they truly cost
My prayer is that in God's great wisdom I will somehow
manage to be as unselfish in Life, as my Mother
was, to the eyes that are watching me!

THE SEA

I have found a special spot I can truly love, a place
of soft land with a warm sun above

A place to laugh and run and play, a place where
each life lives from day to day

There are no busy phones to ring, just wind
and sand and seaweed and things

I think I'll stay here at least the rest of my life, free
from the burdens of struggle and strife

The land is the shore, the water the sea, it's simply
my serenity, like God made it just for me

If every breeze were listened to their whispers would surely say
lay your worries at my feet and watch as I carry them away

In my quiet moments and far from this place I find

I'll venture back frequently if only to the
sweet memories in my mind

SOMEWHERE

Somewhere on this land I roam across this God's green earth

There is a reason for my being, my life, my own self worth

I question often the path I follow the road of my destiny
How have I managed to come this far and still question
whether, "to be"

I have asked the Lord; Do I not fall short
of all that's expected of me
He answered me with gentle rain that
cleansed from heaven above

The warmth in your heart is the Light of my
stars and the wind beneath my dove
For you, my child, are my own creation and perfect in My Love!

A MOTHER'S LOVE
IS ETERNAL

She's made me laugh she's made me cry

She's given me hope and encouragement to try

She's been a dear in many ways, the sun in

the sky on rainy days

She's awaited the calm through a raging fury

She's given her all though tired and weary

She is so much more than a mother to me

She's as wonderful as a best friend could be!

WINTER SNOW

The gentle snow falls quietly covering the earth
beneath it

Capping the rooftops and closing gaps between
tree branches once split

A sight to take one's breath away her mountains
majesty with white crown fit

This winter land of natural wonder if only cherished for a bit

Will last forever in one's mind's eye as
the peace of God's great wit!

THE FIELD

Once browned with weeds and dried with thorns

The field was abandoned and looked on with scorn

It withered and died from lack of care

For no one bothered with its misery to share

The rain came swift and the sun brought light

The field became green and glistened with might

It now shares its beauty and Love with all

Reminding us that on God's earth no challenge
is too great or small!

FIRST TEACHER

Tiny little faces with eyes wide and all aglow, why
are they all mine Lord, what magic do I know

I vowed to always serve you Lord in every path I take but
why give me the children what difference can I make

I have them only for a while then they're on to someone
new I fear they won't remember me or what I strive to do

And still somehow, I'm drawn without need of any
praise to all the little faces I pray I can help raise

"You are the teacher of my lambs and your work is
not in vain, for the Love I've given them through
you in their hearts will always remain

You have taught them strength and courage and
to face their many fears and instilled in them my
Love that will last through all of their years".

A BLESSING IN DISGUISE

Oh, gentle sky of darkening clouds your
presence impending doom
Quiet now in hollow silence yet rage simmering within

Your starlight muffled by a thunderous haze, you loom

Then your voice bounds out in striking
bolts, your fury now begins

And in the calm of your wakening a rain giving new life in bloom

A blessing in disguise you cleansed the soul of man from sin

God in His Kingdom celebrates as His Angels ready a room

For another lamb is coming home out of the lion's den

Oh, gentle sky of sunshine bright your chores you now resume

To lighten the sorrow of those left behind
and broken hearts to mend.

TEACHER OF LAMBS

You are the challenger not the challenged and
every true victory is given not won!

BE YOU

Be you good or evil there will always be Love

Be you happy or sad there will always be Faith

Be you lost or found there will always be Jesus

MY LIFE

Jesus is my life, my love and my way; He loves
me, He leads me; I love Him, I follow!

PEACE OF MIND

I cannot bring the past to present nor change the hands of time

I cannot tell my futures path nor make reason of life's rhyme

I have though prayed, for at journeys end, a gentle
Peace of Mind

To know of the Joy and Love I have shared
with those I leave behind.

NOW I AM LIVING

I saw the world in a different light when I
found myself in a struggling plight

I learned to look at things with care that someday
they might not be there

I found a way to smile through tears and somehow
at least to challenge my fears

I have seen life dim with end in sight and
through the pain I have seen the light

I now cherish each day of loving and giving, that
more than mere life, now I am living!

I LOOKED UPON THE WORLD

I looked upon the world today and found myself
in great dismay

For how could I have missed before this
beauty of earth and sky and shore

It puzzles me now beyond reason or rhyme how
things I saw different in earlier time

Now that I am blinded by nature's decision, I have
somehow found much greater a vision

That which beholds more than life's given start

Sight not from mine eyes but Love in my Heart!

NO STONE UNTHROWN

Look at me, look in my eyes, take note of all my flaws; speak
your mind of all you see there's no need for which to pause
Count my imperfections, let them ring aloud, I have
earned each one acquired although I am not proud
Scoff at my attire and make mention of literal
simplicities I so apparently lack; then stack your
thoughts of hateful pain so swiftly on my back
There, the job is quite complete, you have left
no stone unthrown; the shell of my humanity
was judged yet goes unknown

Within the eyes beneath the shell there dwells the heart
where lives the soul that sees the light of a savior's toll
I too had sought with eyes of worldly desire I
painfully learned to own my sin, that by Christ's
suffering death I too might live again
Look if you will but understand what you see, for
tis but the *soul* of every man that lives eternally!!

FIFTY RINGS

Look upon this tree oh Lord, it was planted in your name... When
blessed with everlasting love once two became the same
Look upon the branches Lord, they have stretched
and immensely grown... Reaching for eternal
life as by example they were shown
Strong and independent now these branches have bore
sweet fruits... Remembering always the sweat and
tears that when young had nurtured their roots
Look upon each knot and scar though only visible
to the heart... For each one represents an answered
prayer that again new growth would start
Look upon this tree oh Lord and count it's fifty rings... For in
each one through Love and tears your glorious Name still sings
Look upon these planters Lord as they marvel at their
deed... How through Faith, Love and understanding
you have met their every need!
Look upon their hearts oh Lord and see the traces of your
word... Many trials come and gone, yet remembering
faithfully what they heard
"Where two have come before me, you go from here as one, take
this seed and trust me always for I promise My Will be done!"
Look upon their lives oh Lord, the seed nurtured in your way;
the blessing, the tree of family gathered before them here today
In sweet wisdom now oh Lord, acquired through suffering and
pain, May they see in every heart their effort was not in vain...
Remind them oft, of your promise, oh Lord and the gift
of your beloved Son... and that from this day forward
the reap of their harvest, has "only just begin!"

HOW GREAT THOU ART

In the quiet moments sometimes, I realize how close I am to God, yet in my darkest moments I always seem to forget... I'm seeking a wisdom or faith or peace that will withstand those dark moments and keep me always close to God. I can look back into my darkness and see how God held me in His arms yet in the time of darkness I couldn't feel His presence. I am learning how much I love God and just how much I need Him. I am realizing it's okay to need Him all the time and I don't have to try to be strong and independent of Him. He knows I am weak and He is always there whether I choose to acknowledge Him or not, is up to me! Knowing His love, I am ashamed that I have too many times chose not to acknowledge Him answering my own question, why am I alone in this darkness? How many tears have I then added to His sorrows by ignoring Him after He gave everything to me, including His Life! I cannot begin to describe my gratefulness at such an awesome and undeserved gift yet it seems every chance I have had to show my gratitude for this Love of His, I cannot even seem to muster enough faith to trust Him to take care of me as He promised He would... I guess my knowledge of my unworthiness just will not let my human brain comprehend what my heart and soul know as the truth; He would not have given a Son's life up for my sins only to mock that Son by dishonoring His words! How great thou art! I am grateful for my new found hope for myself and others who realize we will forget from time to time but our Father already knows our steps before we even take them and He waits with love and patience to carry us through the falls and soar with us through the joys!

START ANEW

I said a special prayer today that the Lord
would help me find my way

He brought to mind memories of both good times and
bad and helped me recall more were happy than sad

I have truly lost count of all things learned yet remember
each hand that to help me, turned

I follow a heart to which I must be true to venture
out and start anew

And in my Heart now lies this prayer written with
love for those who taught me whilst there

May your lives be fulfilled with all of your dreams
and love be as fluent as rocky mountain streams

May your hopes be bound by a faith unbroken and May
your smiles remain such that words need not be spoken

And in your hearts may you often recall that
once upon a time a team were, we all!

MEDITATION

I began my meditation with asking our Lord to enter my heart, my soul, my mind and my body; I asked for healing and strength and forgiveness. I asked God to keep me unto Him despite myself. I have found my "connection" with God; I realized that "man cannot live by bread alone" is so, so very true! God is all powerful. He is our source of power, when we go to Him in prayer, we are connecting our spirit with Him re-charging our soul's strength.... If and ultimately when all of us one by one, because of temptation, do not go to Him and draw spiritual and soulful power and strength from Him our lives begin to diminish, we become weaker and weaker and struggle and suffer!!! He tells us He is not the author of confusion... He tells us He is all powerful. I have learned, after the struggle, that He is loving and giving and even forgiving of my weakness. I have in the past, and hopefully not in the future, had the habit to not go regularly to "draw strength" from God because when I feel strong, temptation gives me a false sense of security and foolish self-pride... I step out on the tight-rope and halfway through realize I'm not as strong as I thought... Then God reaches out His hand and waits patiently for me to grab hold, saving me once again from myself...my humanness. God is so good! I love Him so much, what a gift God gives to each and every one of us, our individuality and His strength to watch it blossom. Every one of us a drop of His love seeping through time ultimately joining and becoming one in the flowing sea of His Love!

GRANT THEM JOY

Dear Lord I ask you grant them Joy in every single day

Grant them courage to conquer fear and
light to guide their way

Grant them health and prosperity and
guard them from dismay

Grant them Faith in one another that
will never lead them stray

But most of all please grant them Love
through all their lives I pray.   Amen

PROMISE ME

Promise me it will always stay as wonderful as it was today

Promise me you will always share the wonderful
way you love and care

Promise me you will tell everything no matter
what the outcome may bring

Promise me in sickness and health together
we'll suffer or share the wealth

Promise me your Love forever true for all
of these things I promise you!

DADDY'S HAND

The hand that used to cradle me
The hand that held me tight
The hand that set me straight
And taught me wrong from right
The hand that used to lead me
The hand that nursed me well
The hand that gently pulled me up
Each and every time I fell
The hand that had to disagree
The hand that had to let go
The hand that waived good-bye
To me yet never felt it so
The hand that I'm still holding
In every single prayer
The hand that I still reach for
And always find it there!
Daddy's Hand

SECOND BEST

He brings the morning sun that's full of cheer and fun

He brings the evening light that makes everything alright

He offers a tender kiss that can raise a fallen star

He sends his love to find me when ere I wander far

He fills my life with such a joy that the world could never mar

He tells me oft that in his heart, I am second to his car!

DEAREST FRIEND

Dearest friend this is a heartfelt wish for a world of dreams come true, for laughter through tears and sunshine through rain, for a hand to hold onto through all of life's pain, for a gentle suggestion or the will to refrain, for a helping hand or an ear to complain. I stop and look in retrospect at how truly lucky I've been for I have known all of these things ever since I called you friend!!

MY LOVE

How sweet love can be when given straight from the heart

God only knows how much I've loved
you dear from the start

I watch you quietly and absorb your charms,
how sweet my dream of being in your arms

I can see inside this soul I love and his pure
light is strength from above

Gentle and strong with passion to abound, eyes
that speak clearly without making a sound

Please love, walk slowly in life let not your dreams
hollow, for quietly in the distance my heart will follow!

SUMMER RAIN

Whence there comes in a summer rain the sultry
quiet of a blue terrain

There my heart waits steadfast and true if for
only a chance to be taken by you!

THE HERO

The hero is a mighty soul that many
seek in times of trial, to take away all
that is evil and give them back a
contented smile..
The hero is a steadfast soul that many
know they'll never find for, to many, a hero
is untouchable beyond the dreams in
their mind..
For me the hero is a soul who never looked
away, but kept the light on constantly for
others to see their way...
For me, the hero is not a dream, it is
a gift of love ever true, for me the hero
is the heart and soul that lives
inside of you!

FINAL CURTAIN

Dear Lord I asked for sunshine but all I see is rain
I asked for health and happiness but somehow find only pain
I asked for peace of heart and soul but still I am uncertain
I asked for healing in the Love of my life and instead
saw a final curtain
Dear Lord I ask you one more thing, please gently tell me why?
As I stood alone with a broken heart and no more tears to cry
A rush of warmth I had never known came and encircled me
"The rain you've seen has cleansed a soul and set a sufferer free
I assure you the peace your loved one now
holds is in answer to your prayer
I have always stood at the door to your heart hoping
you'd notice me there
In the past I have shared your pain giving the answers
you could no longer hear

But now we walk together again forever that
in life and death you needn't fear"...

GRANDPY

We look at him through tiny eyes that are always on the go
Searching for a new adventure that sometimes
makes him say no-no!
We question him in every way to prove that he is right
For as little as our bodies are, we are just as full of might!
We sometimes cross the boundaries that are set-up in the start
By using that secret weapon; the key we hold to his heart
We learn from him so many things that only time brings clear
And as we grow, we appreciate him much
more from year to year
We are sometimes not so graceful in the things we say and do
Like the way we try expressing how
much Love we have for you
We ask that you take each day of our youth
with a little laughter and stride
For with your help and a little luck, we will someday
earn your pride!

THE ANNIVERSARY GIFT

This jar is like our hearts, full of Love and overflowing

These cushions a touch of the "reap" from a harvest
you've long been sowing

These kisses are sweet memories, count them one by one

They will replenish quickly as each new
day "you've only just begun"

But the greatest gift you have given each other, not husband
or wife or father or mother, not even a grandparent's pride

It's that through all your Love you have not been follower
and leader, but you've always walked side by side!

SWEET MOTHER'S PRIDE

The Lord truly giveth no more than we can bare and he
prays that our anguish we will turn to Him and share

For though our hearts are broken and crying, it is a
greater Peace for our loved one He is trying

Hold your head high and try to smile for she is always
with you in every dark while

Remember her words and the kindness she's shown
for she's given them to you for your very own

Time and distance are the challenge you face for
someday you'll reunite in a wonderful place

Take from her the courage it took to live her life and
the advantage is yours no matter your strife

Give that strength to the child she knew you
carry and go on in life, try not to tarry

For she watches in heaven with sweet Mother's pride
as she lives in your heart and soars by your side!

THE PASTOR

I asked the Lord to give me an example to teach me how to
Love; when all I see are empty faces that judge me just because
I asked the Lord to give me light to help me find a way for
in this world I see the sadness of each one's darkest day
I asked the Lord to give me strength when all
of my efforts fail to ease the burdens of loved
ones with the stories of Him I'd tell

I knelt upon a pew in church and gently asked
for Peace for an end of the sadness and pain in
others, I prayed, "Lord, make it cease!'

I looked up and on the wall before me a light
shone on "HIS" face, a voice said softly," This is
my Son, he's on this cross in your place

Let not your heart be troubled for like Him
you have done a great task; living your life in
search of my Will is all I've ever asked

You have turned to me for light and strength and told
others of my name, because of Him your sins are forgiven,
because of your Faith He did not die in vain!"

THE ROSE

It is the gentle heart that cannot hide it's need to Love felt deep inside......That captures the rose who opens her soul to find the half that makes her whole!

LIKE THE CHILD

Like the child who cleans his room only with Mother's prompting.... Must God appear before us with pointed finger and ask, "Are you not fed well while your brother hungers? Is your Faith in me so slight that you cannot Trust that if you share your abundance then neither of you will starve?"

Faith grows with Trust and Trust begins Love, then Love feeds the Soul... The Soul, our candle light in Heaven's window, awaiting us to find our way home!

POP

I fell asleep, it's been years ago now and followed the light in my dream... It led me down the path of my life where in my body was weightless it seemed

The further I traveled my heart became light and my soul was like never before free... The place I came to was perfect in every way, no pain, no struggle, no want, just heavenly as far as I could see!

I felt so calm and warm inside as though I had found the missing peace, I said, "Lord, this dream is so very perfect I wish it would never cease"....

A gentle voice then spoke to me and though startled I listened on, "Welcome home my precious one it's been so very long" ....

Slowly my eyes began to tear as the picture He showed me became gently clear.... All of my family and friends were gathered, they were crying and deeply distressed for they felt that they had said good-bye forever when they laid my body to rest....

I was saddened for them as they were for me, if only I could share my blessed reality!

The Lord said, "Do not worry for I will comfort them too, I will replace their pain with sweet memories of you"

Time for them seems to linger on and I see I still live in their hearts.... My hope is rewarded every day of their journey, for at its end is when Life really starts!

JOYOUS THANKSGIVING

I said a prayer to the Lord today, to thank Him
for the Blessings He's sent my way

Among these Blessings I included your name, for
without your Love my life wouldn't be the same

I have asked the Lord to bring unto you all that
He has promised a heart just and true

For in His light, my friend, we are living and no greater
a gift is worth more Joyous Thanksgiving!

WRITER OF HEART

I am a writer of heart not degree, so here
I must start if ever "to be!" .....

GOD BLESS THE HOUSE

God Bless the House that is made a home
through love and warmth and sharing

God Bless the heart that is made His own
through joy and Peace and Caring

God Bless the people who have made a family
through sadness and trial and daring

God Bless our minds that are given Peace through
His suffering death our sparing!

ELIZABETH

Dearest one with eyes of blue and heart of gold
this is sent to you as a story told

Once upon a time a while ago a life was
given that had a special glow

It glimmered in the darkness so that all could
see, Life is truly what you make it to be

It has withstood the sadness that others couldn't
bear and always managed it's love to share

It has offered strength when others are weary
with a ray of sunshine bright and cheery

It has weathered this world for 75 years in glorious
victory through laughter and tears

This life is endless with no final chapter for
all of God's angels live life ever after

Thank you, Lord, for no greater a gift this family
hath, then our very own Laura Elizabeth!

MUMMA

There are so few special people in this world today who still reach out to others and help them along the way...

There are so few who stand in the shadows and strive not for all the glory, but praise the Lord in His great wisdom for the writing of their life story

The Lord said upon His earth so troubled, He would send a chosen few, to lead the others out of darkness by giving them hope anew...

We celebrate this day, your birthday, as a gift from God above for He gave to us one of His chosen in whom we've all found Hope and Love!!

DON'T HIDE YOUR LOVE

Don't hide your Love, for a love shared is a love gained!

NEVER LEAVE

Never leave a friend in need of help because you can't find the right words; for your presence assures the presence of God and the presence of God assures an answer!

OUR WEDDING DAY

The sun rose high and the birds all sang

The breeze blew soft and the church bells rang

Together we stood attentive and proud

Together we greeted the upgrowing crowd

The excitement did grow as the time came near

The fears did cease as our lives formed clear

Hand in hand we listened with care

The words about life the priest did share

Kneeling in prayer for God's mighty Love

A Blessing was given to us from above

Now we are one in the life we will lead

Together we'll stand in all of our needs

With our love now bonded so strong and true

The challenge is happiness in our life anew.

THE LAST TEAR'S FOR YOU

It's true I've been in love before and found it to be quite nice

But it's you the one I'll always adore no matter what your vice

My love has been given a time or two but
only for one was it right

My heart, my Love, I give to you for you
hold the key to lock it tight

I often sit now debating on what I could have missed

And I only come up waiting for the last
time by you I'll be kissed

Now it all seems so far away that day you choose to go

I know not just what to say, except I still Love you so...

My Love, my Dear, was oh so true but the
day has come for me to depart

The last of my tears are all for you, you'll find
them when you unlock my heart

HEART AND SOUL

It seems to have taken me years to get to this place inside, this place where heart and soul have connected and I am at last a whole person not yet perfect but aware of my existence. I yearn for a closeness to my Father that this earth constantly dangles in front of me then snaps away at my near grasp of it. Is it then that I have failed the test of perseverance? I have missed the wisdom our Savior came to this earth to personally teach us? What greater pain than to finally realize what joy there is in the gifts our Father gives us only to also realize how undeserving I am of them. To try and try again only to be reassured that I am a sinner. Oh what truly must have been the great "Patience of Job!" I pray our beloved Lord God, Father of all creation, be merciful unto us, grant us your undying Love, keep high our hopes and joys that we may recall them in our minds each time we stumble over our faults, let not our hearts be heavy but wash us clean with the body and blood of our precious Savior. Hear me oh Lord I pray, hear me! For I believe the blood of your beloved Son is the most precious gift anyone has ever given me and I truly know in my heart that there is nothing of this world or we humans' capabilities that His blood cannot wash clean. My pain, oh Lord, is knowing that each day I have again made it necessary for His blood to be shed on my behalf! Yet each day I am refreshed by Your tender mercies and Great love, I step out into the world with high expectations and unfathomable hopes. I ask for you to show me your Will that I may reach for it and how rewarded I have been in the many, many prayers you have answered favorably on my behalf. Oh Lord, I dedicate my heart, soul, mind and body to you; Please teach me to be more like you! I am a parent that truly still needs to be parented, as I am a child who still really wants to be loved! I feel as though I have been taken from my home and placed here, this wonderful place of freedom to experience all that I am capable of both good and bad, yet inside I now know here is not home and this lost feeling is the only true Home Sickness we believers shall know. I suppose we must take up the "Cross" as Jesus did, and work diligently for our Father who has entrusted us with His great Faith and Love to do so... When I think of Him asking me to seek Him in every place, I find that when doing so I can see Him everywhere, in everything and in everyone! He truly has many shapes, many faces and many tongues that wherest I go, He is there also! Thank you Father for this gift of sight that I was "born" with and have through your grace learned truly how to see. I dedicate this thought to my Mother, who was a wonderful example of a life dedicated to our Father and the great rewards of living for Him; she taught me through her actions that every challenge is a gift from God, a chance to save a lost soul through the sharing of Faith. She praised Him until her earthly death and I praise Him for her eternal Life!

BLESSINGS TO YOU ALL!

www.ingramcontent.com/pod-product-compliance
Lightning Source LLC
Chambersburg PA
CBHW071452150726
48000CB00006B/2541